David and His Friend, Jonathan

The story of two Old Testament friends
1 Samuel 19–20 for children

Written by Julie Dietrich
Illustrated by Marcy Ramsey

Arch® Books Copyright © 2005 Concordia Publishing House, 3558 S. Jefferson Avenue, St. Louis, MO 63118-3968   1-800-325-3040 • www.cph.org

Manufactured in Colombia

Picture a friend, your very best friend,
One who would stick with you right to the end.
Hours of talking, plenty of playing;
Side-by-side is where you'd be staying.

Years ago, in the days of King Saul,
Two friends, just like this, lived in the king's hall.
One named Jonathan, who happened to be
The son of King Saul—a prince naturally.

Jonathan's friend, David, lived there too.
King Saul watched everything they would do.
The two young friends didn't seem to mind.
They became best buddies, two of a kind.

The Lord called David from up above
To guide His people and lead them with love.
Crowds of people would cheer and shout.
It appeared to be David they cared about.

King Saul kept watching and decided to be
Jealous of David. He looked carefully
For ways to make himself look better;
Saul chose to deal with this little go-getter!

David saw what King Saul was doing:
Ranting and raving, pacing and stewing.
David knew he must come up with a plan.
He'd rely on God's help to quiet this man.

Jonathan couldn't believe his ears
When David shared his concerns and his fears.
His father, jealous of David? No way!
The same friend he talked with day after day?

Yes, it was true. So the two friends began
To put things in motion and start up their plan.
Whatever would happen they both knew one thing:
God would be with them; help He would bring.

The very next day the boys went to a field.
Here David would hide, God being his shield.
David promised to wait near Ezel, a stone.
Jonathan hated to leave his friend all alone.

If King Saul's anger showed up the next day,
Jonathan would return and come up with a way
To let his friend know whether to stay or to run.
They would follow the Lord; God's will be done.

Jonathan returned to face his dad.
Dinner was served, but King Saul seemed mad.
Where was David? He wanted to know.
His face turned red; he looked ready to blow!

Jonathan ran as fast as he could
Back to the field, like he said he would.
His servant came, and three arrows were shot.
Past David they landed; the message he got.

If the arrows had landed in front of the stone,
David knew it would be safe for him to go home.
But they didn't, and so the message was clear:
David knew he must leave and not reappear.

The two friends hugged; tears began to flow.
Jonathan said, "Go in peace, friend, go!"
Both walked away, never looking behind.
They'd remain best buddies—two of a kind.

God kept this friendship alive so we'd see
His plan of salvation for you and for me.
For through David's family a Savior He'd send
His promised Redeemer, our very best Friend.

God blessed us with the Friend who would
Die for our sins, suffering for our good.
He rose from the dead three days later.
Jesus did that for you—no love is greater!

Picture your Friend, your very best Friend.
Jesus will stick with you right to the end.
Hours of talking—He listens to prayer.
Right by your side, He'll always be there.

Dear Parents,

It's easy to picture the two friends in this well-known Old Testament story. David and Jonathan can easily be described as two pals, best buddies to the end. Despite the jealousy and dislike Jonathan's father had for David, nothing or no one could stand in the way of their friendship. God truly blessed David and Jonathan with an exceptional gift of companionship.

An even more significant friendship has been granted to each of us. God used this special friendship to bring Jesus into the world. Jesus came from the house and lineage of David. This is how God gave His Son, Jesus Christ, to be our best and closest Friend. This Friend is our God and our Savior. Jesus is the Friend who will always be there, never leaving us behind. Jesus showed His exceptional love and friendship the day He died on the cross for our sins. "Greater love has no one than this, that he lay down his life for his friends" (John 15:13). Jesus Christ's death on the cross forever defeated Satan, our enemy, who would like nothing more than to see our friendship with our Savior ended. Only by God's grace through faith in Jesus can the forgiveness of our sins and the promise of heaven be ours. This wonderful gift of grace and faith comes through God's Holy Word.

All parents want the best for their children, including the companionship and devotion of friends. Those who belong to the family of God don't need to worry if their child will have a best friend. That's already been taken care of—Jesus Christ promises to be a Friend and Savior to all. Say a prayer with your children, thanking Jesus for the unconditional forgiveness, love, and friendship He gives to them.

The Author